SCIENCE
ESSENTIALS
PHYSICS

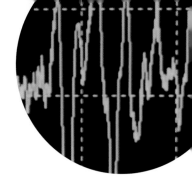

Sound and Vibrations

GERARD CHESHIRE

Evans

EVANS
LONDON

© Evans Brothers Ltd 2006

Published by:
Evans Brothers
2a Portman Mansions
Chiltern Street
London W1U 6NR

Series editor:
Harriet Brown

Editor:
Katie Harker

Design:
Robert Walster

Illustrations:
Peter Bull Art Studio

Printed in China by
WKT Company Limited

British Library Cataloguing in
Publication Data

Cheshire, Gerard, 1965-
  Sound. - (Science essentials.
  Physics)
  1.Sound - Juvenile literature
  I.Title
  534

ISBN-10: 0237530082
13-digit ISBN (from 1 January 2007)
978 0 23753008 2

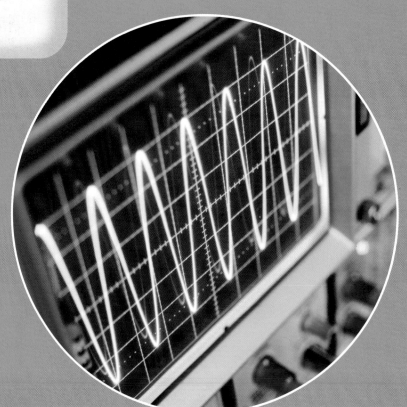

Contents

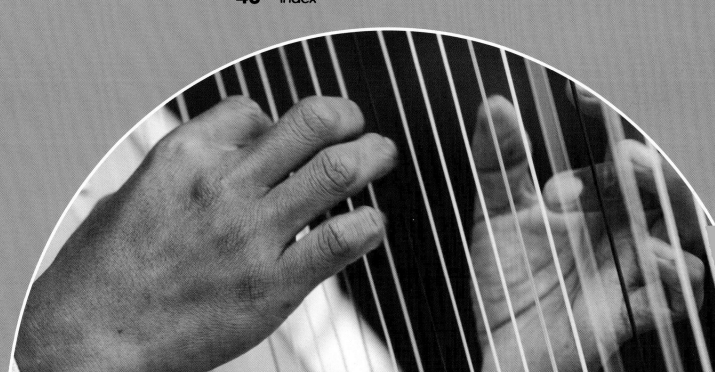

Introduction

Sounds are a part of our everyday lives and help us to make sense of the world around us. We use sounds to communicate, to warn of danger and as a source of entertainment.

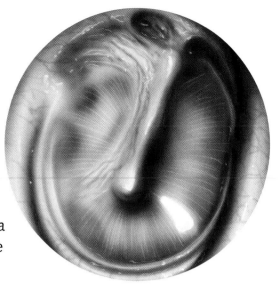

This book takes you on a journey to discover more about the wonderful world of sound and vibrations. Learn how sounds are made. Discover the hearing mechanism of the ear that enables us to interpret sounds, and look at the different ways in which sound can be recorded and replayed. You can also find out about famous scientists, like Francis Hauksbee and Hermann von Helmholtz. Learn how they used their skills to discover how sounds are produced and how we detect the noises around us.

This book also contains feature boxes that will help you to unravel more about the mysteries of sound and vibrations. Test yourself on what you have learnt so far; investigate some of the concepts discussed; find out more key facts; and discover some of the scientific findings of the past and how these might be utilised in the future.

Sounds are a vital part of our daily lives. Now you can understand more about the science behind the sounds that you hear.

DID YOU KNOW?

▶ Watch out for these boxes – they contain surprising and fascinating facts about sound and vibrations.

TEST YOURSELF

▶ Use these boxes to see how much you've learnt. Try to answer the questions without looking at the book, but take a look if you are really stuck.

INVESTIGATE

▶ These boxes contain experiments that you can carry out at home. The equipment you will need is usually cheap and easy to find.

TIME TRAVEL

▶ These boxes describe scientific discoveries from the past, and fascinating developments that pave the way for the advance of science in the future.

ANSWERS

At the end of this book on page 46, you will find the answers to questions from the 'Test yourself' and 'Investigate' boxes.

GLOSSARY

Words highlighted in **bold** are described in detail in the glossary on pages 46 and 47.

What is sound?

Sounds are all around us. When we wake we hear the sounds of daily life; when we walk we hear footsteps; and when we talk we communicate sounds with others. Sounds help us to make sense of the world and to express our ideas. Understanding sounds can also keep us out of danger. Sounds are a part of our everyday lives, but we seldom stop to think about what sound is and how it works.

GOOD VIBRATIONS

Sounds are produced when an object **vibrates**. This object might be vibrating within a solid (such as metal), a liquid (such as water) or a gas (such as air). Most of the time, the sounds that we hear are travelling through air. When an object vibrates the air particles around it are forced to move. When you strike a drum or clang a bell, for example, the vibrations of these objects move the air particles surrounding them. The vibrations are then passed from one air particle to the next and eventually reach our ears. The vibration pulses travelling through the air are known as 'sound waves'.

SOUND WAVES

Sound waves are made by air particles being pushed closer together and then spreading apart. When an object vibrates to the right, it pushes nearby air particles closer together. This is known as '**compression**'. The air particles then collide with the particles next to them and so the process goes on. When the object vibrates back to the left, the air particles are able to spread out again. This is called '**rarefraction**'. The repetition of this squeezing and relaxing makes sound waves.

◀ The buzzing sound of a bee is caused by the vibration of its wings. Scientists have calculated that a bee's wings can beat over 250 times a second.

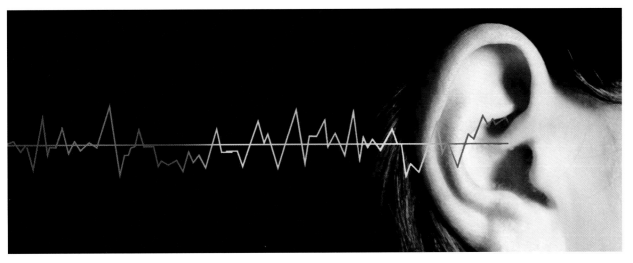

▲ When sound waves reach our ears, they are converted into nerve impulses that the brain can interpret as sound.

Sound waves are known as '**longitudinal**' waves because the particles move in a direction that is parallel to the movement of the waves. Longitudinal waves can also be seen in the muscle contractions of the throat, causing food to travel along when we swallow, or the way in which earthworms move by contracting their muscles.

Sound waves differ from **transverse** waves, which occur when particles move in a direction that is perpendicular to the movement of the waves. The movement of a vibrating string is an example of a stationary transverse wave. An example of a moving transverse wave is the sports stadium phenomenon known as the 'Mexican wave', in which spectators stand up and sit down around a sports stadium to create a wave-like movement. Some of the waves that we can see visibly are a combination of both longitudinal and transverse waves. In the ocean or a lake, for example, friction between the air and the water causes surface particles to move in a nearly circular motion (with both parallel and perpendicular movement) forming waves of water.

▲ When these harp strings are plucked, the strings vibrate from left to right but the waves move up and down the string.

▲ Water waves are waves that involve a combination of both longitudinal and transverse motions.

MEASURING SOUND

Sound waves are invisible, but their movement can be compared to other types of wave that we can see, like ocean waves. Scientists measure the length and height of sound waves using an instrument called an **oscilloscope**. These measurements tell us more about the pitch and loudness of sound. We now know, for example, that we hear a variety of sounds because objects vibrate in different ways, producing sounds waves of different lengths and heights.

FREQUENCY

The length of a sound wave shows the frequency (or **pitch**) of the sound. This gives an indication of the number of complete vibrations (or waves) that pass a point each second. The more vibrations per second, the higher the frequency, and the higher the pitch of the sound. Frequency used to be measured in cycles per second (cps) but since the 1960s they have been measured in hertz (Hz), after Heinrich Hertz, a German scientist who studied electromagnetic waves. One hertz is one vibration per second. High-pitched sounds are often measured in 'kilohertz' (a thousand hertz) or 'megahertz' (a million hertz).

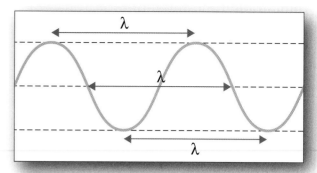

▲ The length of one complete sound wave indicates the frequency (or pitch) of a sound.

Large objects vibrate slowly. The note produced by a large bell will have a low pitch because only a few sound waves are produced per second. A smaller bell will vibrate quickly, producing more sound waves per second and a higher pitch.

▲ Church bells come in different sizes to produce varying pitches of sound.

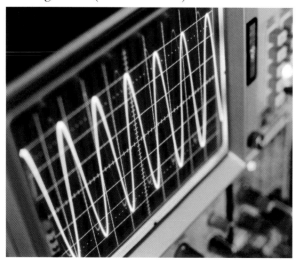

▲ This oscilloscope indicates the frequency (pitch) and amplitude (loudness) of a sound wave.

AMPLITUDE

The height of a sound wave shows the **amplitude** of the sound. This gives an indication of how much energy the wave has (see page 27). Loud sounds produce sound waves that are tall in height. A loud sound can be made by shouting, blowing

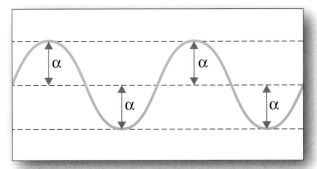

▲ The height of a sound wave indicates the amplitude (or loudness) of a sound.

hard into a wind instrument, plucking a stringed instrument strongly or hitting a drum skin hard. Plucking a string or hitting a drum gently, produces a soft or quiet sound because the vibrations have less amplitude and are smaller in height.

ALARM BELLS

Sound waves are one of the most effective ways of warning people about danger. That is why alarms, whistles, horns and sirens have been used for many years. These devices tend to make unpleasant and loud sounds, to grab our attention

▲ Fire alarms produce loud sounds to warn us of danger.

and to encourage us to take action. Examples include doorbells, bicycle bells, car horns, ship foghorns, air-raid sirens, fire alarms, alarm clocks and emergency vehicle sirens. In recent years, some ambulances have been fitted with multi-phase sirens which produce a series of different sounds. If drivers on the road are listening to car stereos, these sirens are easier to detect, instructing drivers to move over so that the ambulance can pass.

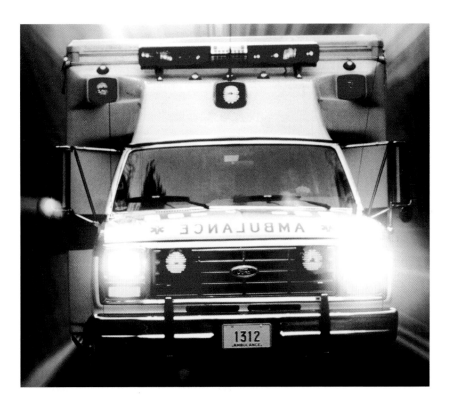

◀ Emergency vehicles use loud sirens to alert pedestrians and other vehicles of their presence, so that they can move quickly through traffic.

In ancient times, people began to notice that sounds or noises travelled at a certain speed. They also realised that the speed of sound and the speed of light were different. This explained why they sometimes saw actions at a distance before they were heard, such as the striking of an axe against a tree, the smoke from a gunshot, or someone diving into water.

SCIENTIFIC INVESTIGATIONS

As early as 550 BCE, the Greek mathematician Pythagoras observed that vibrating strings produced sound and tried to find out why the length of the strings made different tones. However, it wasn't until the 1600s that a study revealed the way in which sound travels. In 1705, British scientist Francis Hauksbee demonstrated that sound needs a material in which to travel. Hauksbee showed that although a bell could be heard ringing when placed in a glass jar, when the air was pumped out of the jar (creating a **vacuum**), the sound could no longer be heard. Hauksbee explained that the sound could only be heard in the first case because the vibrating bell caused the air in the jar to vibrate, which in turn vibrated the jar and then the air particles outside.

▲ We see this diver hit the water before we hear the splash, because light travels faster than sound.

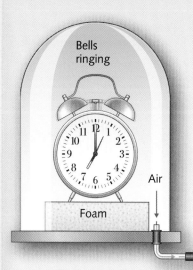

Bells ringing

Air

Foam

Air pump

▲ Hauksbee's bell jar experiment proved that sound waves couldn't travel in a vacuum.

▲ Ernst Chladni

For many years, people puzzled about whether there was a connection between sound, vibrations and physical reality. Then, in the late 1700s, German scientist Ernst Chladni gave a visual representation of sound waves by experimenting with vibrating plates. Chladni covered metal plates with sand and caused them to vibrate by running a violin bow across the edge of the plates. The moving bow caused waves of sand to move across the plates and to be **reflected** back again at the edges. Chladni's experiment showed that the vibrating plates made patterns in the sand which varied according to the frequency of the vibrations, suggesting that sound waves can affect physical matter and that these changes can be repeated.

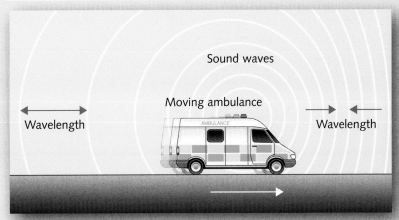

◄ This ambulance's siren causes vibrating air particles to produce sound waves. The ambulance moves slower than the speed of sound, so the sound waves bunch up as the vehicle moves forward, and spread out behind it. As the ambulance approaches, the wavelength is shorter and we hear a higher pitch. As it passes, the wavelength is longer and we hear a lower pitch. This change in pitch is called the Doppler effect.

THE DOPPLER EFFECT

The real proof that sounds were caused by waves came in 1842, when Austrian scientist Christian Doppler noticed that the pitch of sounds changed when their sources moved in relation to the listener. Doppler explained this by suggesting that noises or sounds travelled in waves that become distorted by movement – becoming compressed when their source was travelling towards the ear and stretched when their source was travelling away from the ear. The phenomenon would later become known as the Doppler effect, in his honour.

Imagine walking down a busy main road with a steady stream of traffic. Although the traffic is moving at a constant speed, if you walk in the same direction as the traffic the number of cars (the 'frequency') that pass decreases, and if you walk in the opposite direction the frequency increases. Doppler's theory shows that the same thing happens with sound waves. If we are moving towards a sound (or a sound is moving towards us) we hear an increased frequency (or pitch) because the sound waves get squashed together.

Likewise, if we are moving away (or the sound is moving away) we hear a decreased pitch because the sound waves become stretched apart. This effect is most noticeable when an emergency vehicle drives past with the siren blaring. The noise clearly gets lower when the ambulance or fire engine races past. The same effect occurs if the vehicle is standing still but we move past at speed, in a car for example.

◄ The Doppler effect can be witnessed every time you walk past a steady stream of traffic.

Hearing

Humans and other animals make noises in order to communicate. But they also have extraordinary organs, called ears, which enable them to detect and hear the vibrations of sound waves. Our ears translate the sound waves that they pick up into a type of signal that the brain can understand. Hearing is one of the most important ways in which we can make sense of the world around us.

Ossicles (hammer, anvil and stirrup)

Semicircular canals

Auditory nerve

Auditory canal

Eardrum

Cochlea

Eustachian tube

◄ Our ears have a number of components that help us to detect sound waves. When sound waves reach the ear, they cause the eardrum to vibrate which in turn causes vibrations in the ossicles (ear bones) and the hairs in the cochlea. These movements send messages to the brain via the auditory nerve. Our ears are also linked to the throat via the Eustachian tube.

THE OUTER EAR

Although our senses of smell, taste and vision use chemical reactions to give the brain instructions about the world around us, our sense of hearing is simply a mechanical process. The fleshy growths on the sides of our heads that we call 'ears' are just the outer part of our ear mechanism. Our ears are angled forward and have a number of curves, designed for catching and funneling sound waves so that they can be detected by the middle and inner ears, which sit inside our skulls. Parts of our inner ears sense the movement of air particles and translate them into electrical signals that pass to our brains.

STEREOPHONIC HEARING

In the same way that we have two eyes (to increase our range of vision and to judge distances), we have two ears to detect noise effectively. If we only had one ear it would be difficult to locate the origin of a sound or noise. Sound waves coming from the left reach the left ear a bit sooner (and are also slightly louder) than the sound waves reaching the right ear. Sound waves also reach our ears at different angles and the brain is able to interpret these tiny variations. **Stereophonic** hearing gives us a better sense of the world around us, and can help us to detect potential dangers and to avoid injury. In ancient times, stereophonic hearing was important in helping people to hunt for food, enabling them to pinpoint the noises of animals hidden in undergrowth.

▼ Cinemas use surround sound for a more dramatic effect.

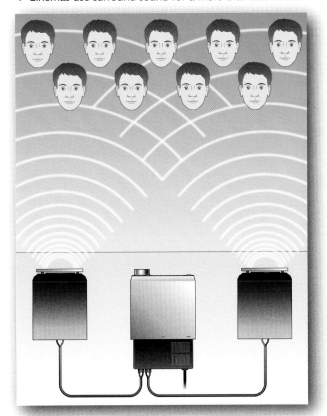

In cinemas today, the surround sound systems make full use of our ability to hear stereophonically. Different speakers in the cinema emit varying parts of the music or dialogue to give us an impression that the sound is coming from all around us. The walls also help to deflect the sound (see page 24).

THE EARDRUM

When sound waves travel down the ear hole they meet a barrier called the tympanum (or 'eardrum'). The eardrum is a thin piece of skin about 10 millimetres wide – a diaphragm of tissue similar to the skin of a drum. It is rigid and very sensitive – vibrating with the slightest movement of air particles. High-pitched sounds move the eardrum quickly, while low pitched sounds move the eardrum slowly. Quiet sounds move the eardrum slightly, while loud sounds move the eardrum a greater distance.

Our ears are connected to the throat via the Eustachian tubes. Air enters the ears from both the outer ear and the mouth and this keeps the pressure on both sides of the eardrum equal. This pressure balance lets the eardrum vibrate freely back and forth. However, sometimes this pressure can change causing our ears to hurt. At high altitude, if we travel in an aeroplane for example, the air pressure changes and the eardrum is pushed outwards and stretched. Sounds become muffled because the eardrum can't vibrate naturally, and the stretching can become painful. Swallowing can help the air pressure to become balanced again.

▼ Illustrated eardrum
(x 10 magnification)

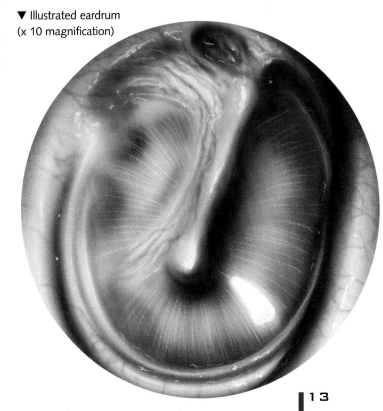

INSIDE THE EARS

Three small bones behind the eardrum – the hammer, stirrup and anvil – are used to increase the strength of the eardrum vibrations and transfer them to the inner ear. The eardrum is connected to the hammer which moves from side to side when the eardrum vibrates. This in turn moves the anvil and the stirrup. The stirrup rests against the cochlea, a spiral shaped cavity in the inner ear that looks like a snail shell. The cochlea is filled with fluid and the moving stirrup acts like a piston, creating waves in this fluid. Once the sound vibrations reach the cochlea they are about 22 times more powerful than the original vibrations of the eardrum.

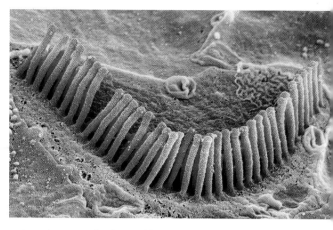

▲ Tiny hairs inside the cochlea (x 21,000 magnification).

The cochlea then takes these physical vibrations and translates them into electrical information that the brain can recognise as sound. Hairs inside the cochlea feel the vibrations and when they move they send an electrical impulse through the auditory nerve. The hairs vibrate at different frequencies, depending on the type of sound wave, and this helps the brain to interpret whether the sound is loud or soft, high or low.

Our ears are an extremely complex design of specific structures, and it's amazing to think that such a small area of the body provides us with a sense of hearing. We still don't know everything about how these structures work, but scientists are making rapid advancements and discovering new elements of hearing all the time. For example, researchers are beginning to make progress in their understanding of how hair cells in the ear transmit signals to the brain.

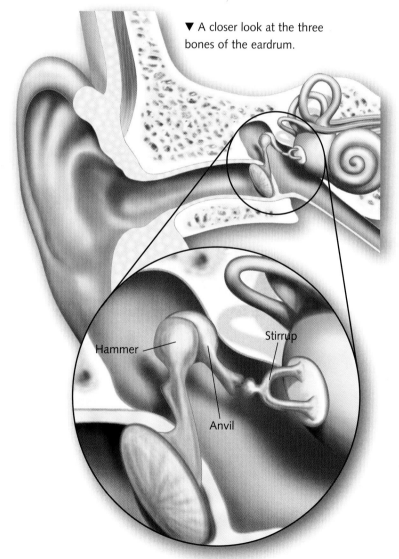

▼ A closer look at the three bones of the eardrum.

Hammer

Stirrup

Anvil

DID YOU KNOW?

▶ Have you ever listened to a recording of your voice and been surprised at the way it sounds? When we speak or sing we hear the sound waves that we make, but we also detect the vibrations travelling through our heads. When we hear a recording, these vibrations have been removed and we think we sound very different.

SOUNDS UNDERWATER

Sound waves travel faster in water than in air (see page 22). However, they become less defined because water particles are more difficult to move than air particles. Sound vibrations can also be felt in water because the water becomes pressurised (instead of becoming compressed, like air particles).

When divers are underwater they communicate with hand signals because human voices and ears are not suited to emitting and sensing noises in water. The ears of all vertebrate animals – mammals, birds, reptiles, amphibians and fish – work in much the same way as the human ear. However, **aquatic** animals have adapted slightly differently because they need to detect sound waves in water rather than air.

▶ These divers are practising hand signals so that they can communicate underwater, without using sounds.

▲ Dolphins have a sharp sense of hearing, despite living mainly underwater.

Marine **mammals** have adapted to communicate underwater. They detect most sound waves through their lower jaw and these vibrations are transferred to their middle and inner ear. Marine mammals also have ear holes (located behind the eyes) that are covered with a layer of skin. Some scientists believe that dolphins and whales can hear low frequency sounds through these ear openings, but it is not known for sure.

Invertebrates (such as grasshoppers, spiders and worms) hear sounds and vibrations in a variety of different ways. Grasshoppers have a special hearing organ on the first segment of their abdomen. Crickets have a similar hearing organ which is located on their front legs. These special organs convert sound waves into vibrations (rather like the human eardrum), sending a response to the brain. Other invertebrates use their whole bodies to detect sounds and vibrations – spiders, for example, sense changes in the fluid pressure within their body caused by the energy of sound waves (in much the same way that we can feel vibrations with our hands). Earthworms have a thin, sensitive skin which enables them to detect changes in light, temperature, moisture and vibration. Worms will move away from a source of vibration, to protect themselves from danger.

Invertebrates communicate sounds in unique ways, too. Grasshoppers produce a high-pitched 'chirping' sound by scraping their hind legs against their wing or their body. Crickets produce a similar sound by rubbing their wings together.

▲ Crickets have hearing organs on their front legs, and communicate sounds by rubbing their wings together.

Male fiddler crabs produce sounds by banging their large claw against the sand to warn others that a predator is coming. Fiddler crabs don't have a specific hearing mechanism, but they can sense the vibrations alerting them to danger. The male crabs also use these same vibrations to attract a female mate.

A sharp sense of hearing enables animals to detect their predators and also to navigate their way around. Some animals, such as mice or rabbits, rely heavily on their sense of hearing for survival and have adapted over the years to have large outer ears that move to catch as many sound waves as possible. Most rabbits have large, erect ears which move forward or backward as they attempt to pinpoint danger. Rabbits can also hear the high-pitched sounds of some enemies, such as rodents, bats and birds.

◀ Rabbit hearing is extremely sensitive. The rabbit's large ears help it to detect minute sounds that could warn of predators.

In comparison, human ears are relatively small. Our ears also face forward so we tend to hear sounds in front of us better than those behind. Many animals, however, have ears that can focus on sounds from a particular direction. Owls, for example, have a highly developed hearing system because they are active at night when they mainly hunt by sound, rather than sight. Owls have an area of very short feathers (called a 'facial disk') arranged in a rounded pattern on the front of their heads. The facial disk helps collect sounds by funneling them to ears that are hidden beneath feathers at the edge of the disk.

An owl's hearing is very sensitive at certain frequencies, enabling it to hear even the slightest movement of its prey in leaves or undergrowth. Some owls also have **asymmetrical** ears. One ear is higher than the other, which means that as well as being able to locate a source of noise from left to right (as humans can), owls can also locate how far up or down the noise is. This means that owls can pounce on their prey in total darkness and strike at exactly the right place to make a kill.

▲ An owl's hearing is so good that it can hear a mouse almost a kilometre away.

DID YOU KNOW?

▶ The human ear can detect sound waves ranging from about 20 hertz to 20 kilohertz, but many animals can detect sounds at far higher frequencies. For example, bats can hear the sounds of other bats and insects in excess of 100 kilohertz. Cats (right) and owls can hear the very high-pitched squeals of rodents, which are inaudible to humans. Dogs can also hear high-pitched sounds. Special dog whistles are often used to attract a dog's attention because they produce sounds that only dogs can hear.

DEAFNESS

Deafness is a partial or total lack of hearing and affects many people worldwide. Some people are born deaf while others may have become hard of hearing in later life. The human ear can normally hear frequencies of 20 to 20,000 hertz. A person who cannot hear a sound of 20 decibels in a frequency range of 800 to 1,900 hertz is said to be partially (or totally) deaf.

There are two kinds of deafness. 'Conductive deafness' is caused by a problem with the passage of sound waves from the outer ear to the inner ear. This is often temporary and can be cured. An infection may cause the ear canal to become swollen or blocked so that sound waves are unable to pass through. Earwax can also block the ear canal (although total hearing loss only occurs if around 90 per cent of the ear canal is obstructed). More commonly, a smaller amount of wax may press against the eardrum, making it unable to vibrate. It is also possible for the eardrum to become torn by excessive noise, infection or a foreign body that enters the ear canal, such as a bead, insect or a cotton bud.

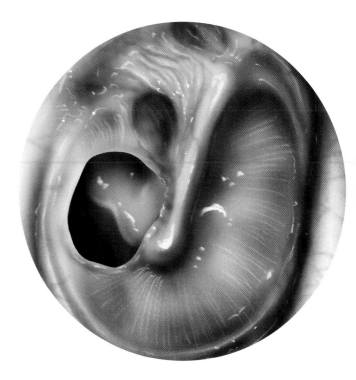

▲ An artist's impression of a perforated eardrum caused by an inflammatory condition, called 'glue ear'.

If the eardrum becomes damaged, sound waves cannot be converted into the vibrations necessary for the bones of the middle ear to transfer the information to the cochlea. A damaged eardrum should heal within a month or so, although more serious cases may require surgery.

'Perceptive deafness' is a more serious condition and is usually permanent. It occurs when there is a problem with the actual hearing mechanism that senses sound vibrations and sends nerve impulses to the brain. Perceptive deafness may be caused by damage to the cochlea, the auditory nerve or the hearing centre of the brain itself. Although people with conductive deafness can usually still hear the sound waves of their own voices travelling through their skulls, those with perceptive deafness hear nothing at all.

◀ Doctors use hearing tests to determine the severity and possible cause of hearing loss.

Infections and hereditary abnormalities can cause both conductive and perceptive deafness. Otitis is a bacterial inflammation that can affect the outer, middle or inner ear. It is treatable with antibiotics but can cause serious and permanent damage, such as tinnitus (a buzzing or whistling in the ear). 'Glue ear', a common complaint in children, is a build up of mucus in the middle ear, caused by otitis. Small tubes, called grommets, can be inserted into the eardrum to allow air to pass through and to drain the mucus. Grommets usually fall out of the ear after a few months, once the infection has passed.

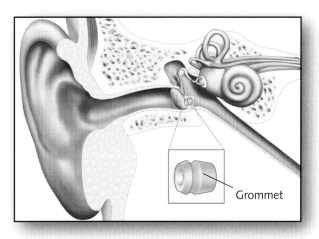

▲ A grommet can be inserted into the eardrum to help drain fluid caused by an infection, and to enable air to flow into the middle ear to improve hearing perception.

Otosclerosis is an inherited condition that causes a gradual overgrowth of the bones in the middle ear, until they no longer function. The condition develops so slowly that many people can be unaware of their hearing loss for some time.

Otosclerosis is painless and if the hearing loss is slight, no treatment may be needed. However, more significant hearing loss may be improved with a hearing aid (see page 20) or surgery may be needed to reconstruct the ear bones.

▲ Sign language is a useful skill that aids communication with people who suffer from hearing loss.

TIME TRAVEL: HEARING DEVICES

The first scientist to study how the ear perceives sound was Hermann von Helmholtz from Germany. Helmholtz believed that we perceive sounds of different pitches because they cause different types of vibrations. In 1857, Helmholtz proposed his 'theory of **resonance**'. He believed that fibres or hairs in the inner ear were tuned to different pitches, so that they resonated (vibrated) to different noises.

Helmholtz's efforts to understand the physical processes of hearing were aided by the work of the New Zealand-born British scientist Ernest Rutherford (1871-1937). Rutherford proposed what became known as the 'telephone theory', which suggested that the cochlea moves in response to sounds, like the diaphragm in the mouthpiece of a telephone (see page 44).

▲ **Hermann von Helmholtz**

▼ **Ernest Rutherford** However, it wasn't until 1961 that Hungarian-born American scientist Georg von Bekesy showed that it was the vibration waves in the fluid of the cochlea that caused the tiny hair-like structures to sense the sounds received by the ear. This is know as Bekesy's 'fluid wave theory'. Bekesy reached his conclusion by using powerful microscopes to observe sound waves in the cochlea.

HEARING AIDS

Today, our knowledge of the hearing mechanisms of the ear has led to the development of hearing aids. These can be worn by partially deaf people to amplify the sound waves received by their outer ear. The first electrical hearing aid was invented in the early 1900s. Before this time, people with partial deafness used an ear trumpet to effectively increase the size of their outer ear so that they could capture more sound waves. Modern hearing aids are battery-powered devices that are small enough to be worn in or around the outer ear. Hearing aids use a microphone to pick up sound waves and covert them into electrical signals. Some use these electrical signals to stimulate the auditory nerve while others amplify the sound before it reaches the inner ear.

▶ **Modern hearing aids are discreetly worn in (or behind) the ear.**

▲ **Ear trumpets were used in the past to improve hearing because they captured more sound waves.**

COCHLEAR IMPLANTS

The groundbreaking research of scientists like Helmholtz and Bekesy helped to explain the biological basis of hearing at a very detailed level. In the late 1900s, researchers took this knowledge and began to look at whether it was possible to create an artificial or 'bionic' ear. In the 1960s, scientists began to develop cochlear implants – small electrical devices that could be implanted in the inner ear. These devices enabled deaf patients to detect simple properties of sound for the first time – they could distinguish speech from non-speech sounds, for example. Then in the 1970s, researchers began to develop and test the multi-electrode cochlear implants which are commonly used today.

Cochlear implants are designed for patients who suffer from profound hearing loss and who gain no benefit from a conventional hearing aid. Patients wear a microphone and processing unit on the side of their head, and a receiver is implanted into the cochlea. Sound waves are picked up by the microphone and are sent through the devices's processing unit to electrodes inside the cochlea. Instead of transmitting sound waves through the fine hairs of the cochlea, the receiver converts sound waves into electrical impulses that transmit messages directly to the auditory nerve.

By the 1990s, the precision and clarity of sound that could be achieved by cochlear implants had greatly improved. Thanks to the devices, many formerly deaf patients can now hear. Today, the technology enables deaf users to carry out a normal conversation. For some patients, cochlear implants have made it possible to communicate over the telephone for the first time. As technology develops, scientists will continue to improve their simulation of the workings of the human ear. In 2004, 54,000 people had received cochlear implants. Children in particular, adapt very well to the devices, because their brains are still learning to interpret sounds. Some children receive a cochlear implant when they are less than 12 months old.

▲ This cochlear implant is being tested on a child. Today, over half of cochlear implant patients are children.

Ways to travel

Sound waves travel at different speeds in different materials. Sound generally travels faster in solids and liquids than in air. This is because the particles in solids and liquids are closer together than in gases so the vibrations travel more quickly.

THE SPEED OF SOUND

The speed of sound in air is about 340 metres per second (that's about ten times the speed of a car in the fast lane of a motorway). In water, sound travels at 1,500 metres per second and in steel it travels at 6,000 metres per second. When we talk about the 'speed of sound' we are usually referring to the speed of sound in air.

Sound waves can't travel in a vacuum where there are no particles (see page 10). In contrast, light doesn't need to travel through a material and moves much faster. Light travels at about 300,000 kilometres per second (about 30 centimetres in a billionth of a second).

▲ Sound travels about ten times faster than the cars on a motorway.

SONIC SOUND

When an aeroplane flies through the sky, the noise of its engines travels at the speed of sound (340 metres per second). Sometimes when we hear an aeroplane from the ground we look up and notice that the sound seems to be coming from a point at some distance behind the aircraft itself. That is because the aeroplane has had time to move forwards before the sound waves have had enough time to travel down to the ground for us to hear them. When an aeroplane's speed is greater than the speed of sound something even more interesting happens. The sound of its engines cannot travel forwards fast enough to escape the plane, so a wall of sound builds up in the form of an air pressure wave. When that wave passes over the ground we hear a loud bang, which is an accumulation of noise from the aircraft. This is called a 'sonic boom'.

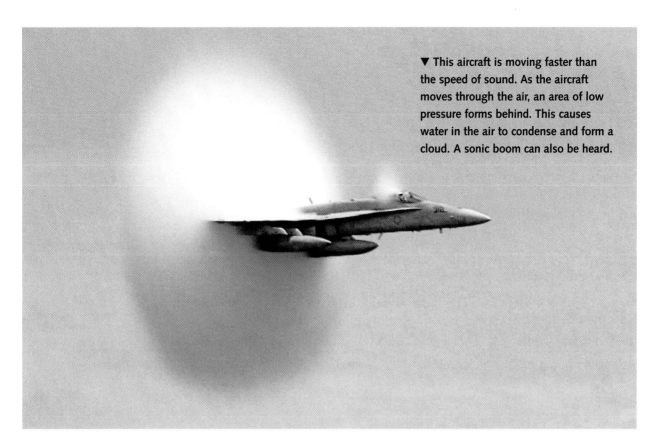

▼ This aircraft is moving faster than the speed of sound. As the aircraft moves through the air, an area of low pressure forms behind. This causes water in the air to condense and form a cloud. A sonic boom can also be heard.

Aeroplanes that travel faster than the speed of sound are described as '**supersonic**'. Supersonic aeroplanes are usually military planes, although space shuttles also re-enter the atmosphere at supersonic speeds. Concorde was the most famous supersonic commercial aircraft but became obsolete in 2003 because of rising costs and safety concerns after a number of accidents. Many countries have laws preventing aircraft from flying at (or above) the speed of sound when they travel over land, to prevent a sonic boom from disturbing the people and animals living there.

DID YOU KNOW?

▶ The 'crack' of a whip is an example of a sonic boom. Whips are used to drive animals because the sound frightens them into moving in a particular direction. A whip is designed so that its diameter becomes smaller towards the tip. When you crack a whip, the energy accelerates down the length so that the tip travels at about 1.3 times the speed of sound. This tiny sonic boom creates the distinctive cracking sound.

REFLECTION AND REFRACTION

When sounds travel through the air they eventually die out because the sound waves spread in different directions and lose their energy. Just as light waves can be reflected or **refracted** by different materials, sound waves can also change direction. When a sound meets an obstacle, some of the sound is reflected back, some is absorbed and some passes through the material.

An **echo** is a sound being reflected off a surface. If we clap our hands, stamp our feet or shout in an enclosed space, such as a small room, we often hear an echo. The sound waves bounce back from the walls and we hear them a fraction of a second after we hear the original sound. In very large

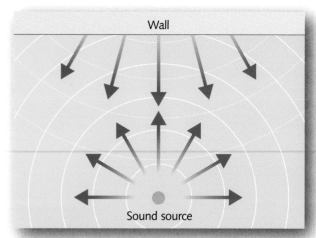

▲ When sound waves meet a surface, such as a wall, some sound waves are reflected and we hear them as an echo.

spaces, such as caves, cliffs or coves, the sound waves may take several seconds to return, so that we hear the echo clearly with no overlap.

Echoes work best against relatively smooth and hard surfaces, such as brick walls, because little energy is absorbed and a lot of sound waves are reflected in one direction. Rough or porous surfaces tend to absorb more sound waves and a weaker sound is reflected because the sound waves bounce back at different angles. A sound echo that is reflected again and again from different surfaces is called a reverberation. The sound becomes weaker with each reflection and eventually becomes inaudible.

▲ Sounds are reflected from cave walls to produce an echo.

INVESTIGATE

▶ Stand about 50-100 metres away from a flat wall and clap your hands. If you notice an echo occurring, begin to clap your hands regularly so that each clap is in time with the echo of the previous one. Count the number of claps that you do in ten seconds. Then, multiply this by twice the distance to the wall (in metres) and divide it by ten (the number of seconds). What is your answer? Turn to page 46 to see if you have correctly calculated the speed of sound in air.

TEST YOURSELF

▶ Why is it not possible for sound waves to travel through a vacuum?
▶ Why do we see the flash of lightning before we hear the sound of thunder?
▶ Put the following materials in the order in which sound waves travel (from fastest to slowest): water, wood, hydrogen.

ABSORBING SOUND

Sound energy is 'absorbed' when it is converted to another form of energy. In most cases sound energy is converted to heat energy because it causes the molecules of a material to start vibrating. Sounds lose energy naturally as they travel through the air because the sound waves thin out, but the sound waves are also absorbed as they collide with air particles. A high-frequency sound fades quickly because its rapid vibrations are quickly converted to heat energy and absorbed. This means that lower frequencies travel further than higher frequencies, and explains why we usually hear the base sounds of a disco far away, but rarely the higher notes of the melody.

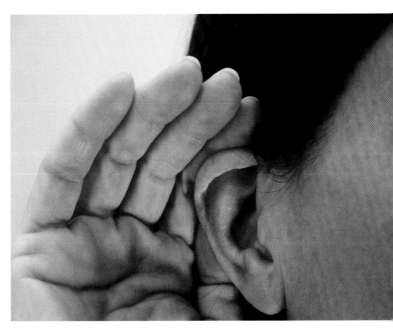

▲ You can increase your sense of hearing by cupping your hand around your ear, to trap more sound waves.

When we hold a seashell to our ear, the shell captures background noise which resonates inside the shell. We can produce the same 'ocean' sound using an empty cup or even by cupping our hand over the ear. Human ears are small compared to some animals, but we can increase our sense of hearing by cupping one hand behind the ear. This helps to funnel more sound waves into the ear.

DID YOU KNOW?

▶ Sound travels further over a frozen lake. As the sound waves travel over the ice they become reflected and refracted by the layers of cold and warm air above the lake. The sound waves keep their energy for longer because they are reflected rather than absorbed.

▶ Furnished rooms echo less than empty rooms. This is because objects in the room absorb and reflect the sound waves so that they have less energy when they reach the walls. Recording studios (right) deliberately break up the surfaces of walls so that echoes are eliminated as far as possible, ensuring a good quality of recording. They also have **insulating** materials on the walls to eliminate any outside sounds that might interfere with recordings.

▶ When music is played outside, the sound travels and eventually fades because there are no surfaces to reflect the sound waves. When music is played inside however, reflections from the walls, ceiling and floor enrich the sound. When an orchestra plays from a stage, the sound reaches the audience directly, but reflections from the walls and the ceiling reach the audience at different angles, giving a feeling that the sound is all around. We now know that the shape of a concert hall influences the music we hear. Too few reflections gives a 'dead' sound but too many can 'cloud' the sound.

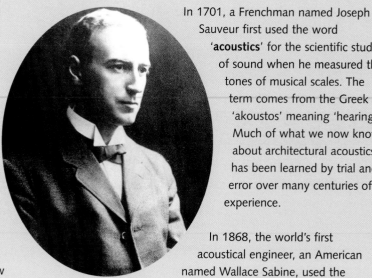

▲ Wallace Sabine

In 1701, a Frenchman named Joseph Sauveur first used the word '**acoustics**' for the scientific study of sound when he measured the tones of musical scales. The term comes from the Greek 'akoustos' meaning 'hearing'. Much of what we now know about architectural acoustics has been learned by trial and error over many centuries of experience.

In 1868, the world's first acoustical engineer, an American named Wallace Sabine, used the principles of his forefathers to design and build the Symphony Hall in Boston, considered to be one of the best concert halls in the world. Sabine recognised that soft surfaces absorb sound, while hard surfaces reflect it. He also studied the way in which different interior surfaces, such as fabrics, wood and plaster, affected the acoustics of a room. The international standard unit of measurement for sound absorption is now called the 'sabin' in his memory.

◀ **The Royal Albert Hall in London is a beautiful building but it was once known for its poor acoustics. The hall used to create many echoes but today, modern acoustic discs (commonly referred to as 'mushrooms') are suspended from the ceiling, helping to absorb any unwanted vibrations.**

Sound energy

Sound waves are vibrations of energy, which push molecules against one another in pulses. When sound waves vary in frequency or amplitude we hear different types and volumes of sound. The intensity or loudness of a noise depends on the amount of energy or power carried by the sound waves – its amplitude. A sound eventually fades because air particles or other obstacles absorb the energy as the sound passes through. This is why noises become less intense at a greater distance or behind a barrier, such as a wall.

NOISE LEVELS

The human ear is extremely sensitive. We can hear everything from the soft sounds of our fingertips rubbing together, to the thumping of a pneumatic drill. Intensity of sound is measured in decibels (dB). Because the range of human hearing is so large, decibels increase in multiples of ten. The smallest audible sound is 0 dB. Ten times more powerful is 10 dB; 100 times more powerful is 20 dB; 1,000 times louder is 30 dB, and so on.

This table shows the sound intensity of various everyday noises. These measurements have been taken near to the source. The intensity will always be less if you are standing further away because some of the energy will have been absorbed.

▼ The varying intensity of everyday noises.

SOUND	INTENSITY
Near total silence	0 dB
Whisper	15 dB
Normal conversation	60 dB
Lawnmower	90 dB
Car horn	110 dB
Rock concert or jet engine	120 dB
Gunshot	140 dB

PAIN THRESHOLD

Have you ever stood next to a loud speaker and found that your ears start tickling? At about 120 decibels we start to feel sound waves as a tickling sensation. At about 130-140 decibels, sound starts to produce pain in the ear as the eardrum is forced to move greater distances. Everyone is different, but the strongest sound that you can tolerate is known as the 'pain threshold'.

▲ Some sounds are so intense that they can hurt the ears.

SOUNDPROOFING

Many types of everyday noise can be reduced using various 'soundproofing' techniques. Builders, architects and engineers try to reduce sound levels in their building projects. Double-glazing is now used in new homes because it helps to save energy, as well as being an effective source of sound-proofing. Glass is a good conductor of both heat and sound vibrations, so a single pane of glass provides very little insulation against heat or sound transmission. Double-glazed windows have a space between two panes of glass. This makes it more difficult for heat or sound energy to pass through. Double-glazing is now required in new buildings to save energy. Many older homes close to busy roads or airports also have double-glazing added as a soundproofing measure.

You can damage your ears if you are constantly subjected to very loud noises, such as machinery or loudspeakers. In noisy factories or building

◀ Protective earphones are now compulsory on many building sites.

▲ Fibreglass insulation laid between floorboards and in the roof can prevent heat loss and act as a sound barrier.

sites, workers wear earphones to protect their ears from intense sound waves. Some machines, such as combustion engines, have silencers (or mufflers) to make them less noisy. In a car exhaust, for example, a metal container with holes and chambers allows combustion gases to expand and sound waves to spread and reflect against different surfaces. Some exhaust systems use fibreglass packing to absorb the sound energy as the gases flow through.

DID YOU KNOW?

▶ Your eardrum helps to protect your inner ear from loud, low-pitch noises. When the brain receives a signal that indicates this sort of noise, a reflex occurs at the eardrum. Muscles in the ear pull the eardrum and it becomes more rigid. As a result, the ear cannot pick up as many noises with a low frequency and high amplitude and the sounds are softened. This effect also helps you to filter out loud low-pitched background noise, enabling you to carry on a conversation when you're in a noisy environment. The reflex also works whenever you start talking, so that the sound of your own voice doesn't drown out the other sounds around you. Despite this clever mechanism, as you get older changes in the inner ear will cause a gradual deterioration in your hearing. In fact, people over the age of 50 are likely to lose some hearing each year. The decline is slow, but may make listening amongst background noise more difficult.

Communication

Birds sing, dogs bark and some snakes rattle. But humans have developed a more sophisticated form of communication – speech. Many different languages are found around the world that enable humans to express their thoughts and feelings. Music has also become an important part of communication. As well as enabling people to convey stories and ideas in a musical form, rhythm, music and song draw people into a common, shared experience.

MUSICAL INSTRUMENTS

Humans have also developed a range of musical instruments that create different types of sounds. These are used for enjoyment and can also express moods and feelings of a different kind. Musical instruments are grouped together according to the ways in which they create their sounds. The main groups are stringed instruments, wind/brass instruments and percussion instruments.

Stringed instruments have a series of strings, which are held taut so that they vibrate to produce sound waves when struck, plucked or brushed (for example, with the fingers or a bow). They include guitars, harps, violins, violas, cellos,

double basses, pianos and harpsichords. In a violin, for example, the bow causes the strings to vibrate and these vibrations are transferred to the hollow wooden body of the instrument via a thin piece of wood called a 'bridge'. The vibrations of the wood, as well as the air in and around the violin, create most of the sound waves. Some of these sound waves eventually escape from the sound holes (or 'f' holes) creating a rich sound. Different sounds are made when the wood vibrates at different frequencies. The pitch of the sound depends on the length, thickness and tension of the string – thin strings have a higher pitch than thick strings, and the pitch gets higher as the string is tightened or shortened. The frequency is also affected by the shape and size of the instrument.

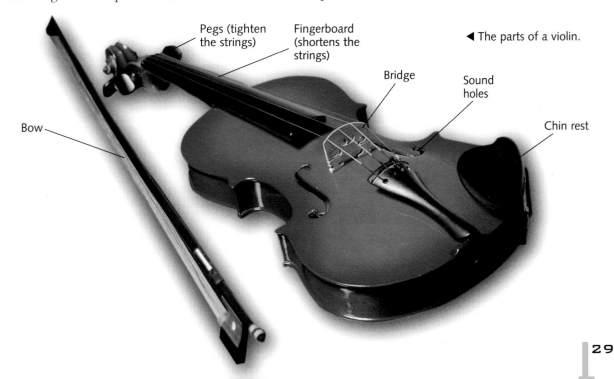

Pegs (tighten the strings)

Fingerboard (shortens the strings)

◀ The parts of a violin.

Bridge

Sound holes

Chin rest

Bow

Wind or brass instruments rely on a flow of air, which is made to vibrate and create sound waves. They include whistles, recorders, flutes, clarinets, trumpets, trombones, tubas, organs, concertinas, bagpipes and harmonicas. The airflow (which is produced by air from the lungs, or from bellows) is made to vibrate by the lips or by a reed as it enters the instrument. Once the air is vibrating, the waves travel through the instrument where the airflow is varied to create different notes. Longer columns of air produce lower notes. At the end of the instrument the tube usually widens to amplify the sound waves as they escape from the instrument.

Percussion instruments rely on sound waves being created by striking a surface. They include drums, cymbals, bells, tubular

◄ Clarinets produce a mellow sound.

bells, xylophones, triangles, glockenspiels, tambourines and tympani drums. A hand, a stick or a hammer is used to strike the instrument, generating vibrations that travel as sound waves through the surrounding air.

TEST YOURSELF

► List these instruments in order of pitch (from high to low) and explain what factors change the pitch of the notes that they make – viola, cello, violin.

▲ From left to right – violin, viola, cello.

▼ Tympani drums can be tuned to particular notes.

COMMUNICATING EMOTION

Listening to music often evokes an emotional reaction of some kind. Many people choose to play music because they want to enhance or to change their mood. Certain elements within music are used to make people feel different emotions.

The speed of music and the mode (major or minor) tend to have the strongest impact – fast music in a major key sounds cheerful, while slow music in a minor key can be sad or sensitive. Fast music is also said to increase your heart and breathing rates while slow music works to reduce them. Sometimes, the flow of the melody causes the listener to have an expectation about how the music might develop. If this expectation is satisfied they may feel positive or relaxed. However, the same music can produce different emotions in a person at different times. Sometimes music simply reminds someone of an experience they have had, or they may just be listening with a feeling of admiration for the performer.

▶ Listening to music is a popular pastime because music tends to enhance your mood.

SPEECH AND SONG IN HUMANS

Humans have an ability to make complex noises, which we describe as talking or speaking. This is a very important skill because it allows us to communicate knowledge, ideas, instructions and feelings about the world in which we live. Without speech we would not have evolved into the civilised beings we are today. But how do we talk?

Our speech mechanism is rather like a wind instrument. Our lungs act as bellows, which send a flow of air between our vocal cords – a pair of opening and closing diaphragms in the larynx, which form a slit in part of the windpipe called the glottis. As the airflow passes through the slit, it causes the edges of the vocal cords to vibrate, so that they produce sound waves. The strength of the airflow from the lungs and the size of the slit determines the pitch and volume of the sounds created. The sound waves then travel from the vocal cords into the mouth. The changing shape of the mouth and the tongue manipulate the sound waves to produce words. Singing works in much the same way, except that the flow of air is more constant. Humming is simply singing but with the lips held closed. Whistling is different though, because the airflow causes the edges of the lips to vibrate instead of the vocal cords.

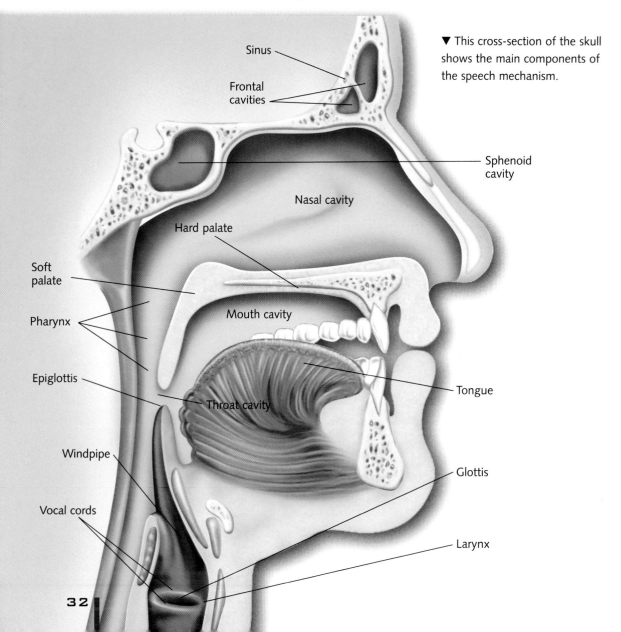

▼ This cross-section of the skull shows the main components of the speech mechanism.

Sinus

Frontal cavities

Sphenoid cavity

Nasal cavity

Hard palate

Soft palate

Pharynx

Mouth cavity

Epiglottis

Throat cavity

Tongue

Windpipe

Glottis

Vocal cords

Larynx

FINDING OUR VOICE

Scientists think that humans began to develop their ability to talk around 100,000 years ago. Before this time, our mouth and larynx had not developed to form words. Although a limited number of words were used at first, the human vocabulary increased over time so that people could express ideas and beliefs to one another, as well as organise groups of people to get things done. At this time, people didn't travel or meet other populations so hundreds of different languages evolved in isolation around the world. Today, there are over 5,000 different languages in the world, although over 90 per cent of these are rarely used today and are likely to become extinct.

▲ The European parliament (above) now has members that span 20 different languages.

▲ At about 14 months of age, children begin to talk by copying their parents.

LEARNING TO TALK, READ AND WRITE

When we are babies we learn to talk by listening to sounds made by those around us until we realise that certain sounds mean particular things. Gradually we practise copying those sounds until people start to understand what we are trying to say. Eventually we get better at understanding the meaning of spoken words and reproducing the sounds ourselves, until we can speak and communicate clearly. The English language is one of a group of languages, known as the Indo-European languages which use alphabets based on the sounds of the words spoken. Any word can be written down by using a combination of letters. Reading and writing are perhaps the best way of recording and reproducing many of the common sounds that we make in order to communicate.

SOUNDS OF OTHER ANIMALS

Many mammals, birds, reptiles and amphibians produce vocal sounds in much the same way as humans, by manipulating a flow of air supplied by the lungs. But there are other ways in which animals make sounds for the purposes of communication. Grasshoppers and crickets are able to 'sing' by rubbing parts of their body together (see page 16). Woodpeckers have strong chiselled beaks which enable them to dig for insects in the trunks of trees and to carve out nest holes in the wood. However, they also use trees as percussion instruments to send drumming sounds through the forests in which they live. Woodpeckers can beat 20 pecks a second to attract attention or to find a mate. A similar behaviour is seen in deathwatch beetles who communicate by striking their bodies against the wood in which they hide. The vibrations then travel as sound waves along tiny tunnels that have been bored into the wood by beetle grubs. Rabbits also thump the ground with their back feet, sending sound waves that are felt as vibrations by other rabbits.

▲ Woodpeckers tap trees as part of their courtship behaviour.

Other creatures use sounds to warn of their presence. Rattlesnakes, for example, warn other creatures to stay away by rapidly shaking specially adapted scales on the ends of their tails. The scales are loosely fitted together so that they rattle against one another and produce vibrations. The vibrations are amplified and move through the air as sound waves because the scales are hollow. A new segment is added to the tail each time the snake sheds its skin. Porcupines are also known to use their tails to ward off predators. The porcupine raises the quills on its back and quivers its tail, to produce a rattling warning sound.

◀ Rattlesnakes have a distinctive sound that deters predators.

Using sound

6

As scientists have begun to discover more about the particular properties of sound waves, others have begun to utilise this knowledge to help in various areas of our lives. Sound waves can travel through gases, liquids and solids and for this reason they now have a wide variety of uses in modern life.

SOUNDING

In times gone by, sailors ensured a safe passage through shallow waters by measuring the depths of the ocean with rods and lines, which were extended until they reached the seabed. This process is called 'sounding' and comes from the Latin word 'subunda' (meaning 'below-waves'). Today, ships are used to make maps of the ocean floor using a system called 'sonar' (sound navigation and ranging). Sonar sends pulses of sound through the water, which bounce back if they meet obstacles, such as the seabed or coral reefs. Knowledge of the Doppler effect (see page 11) is also now combined with sonar technology to determine whether objects in the water are moving towards or away from the ship, and how fast they are travelling.

▲ This researcher is lowering a sonar probe into the ocean to map the seabed.

SEISMIC SURVEYING

Sound waves can also be used to survey geological features hidden below ground. This method – called 'seismic surveying' – is used to determine the structure of the ground, especially when searching for pockets of natural gas, coal and oil. Like the sonar methods used to map depths under water, a similar principle is used with rock (although sound waves need more energy to travel through the ground than through water).

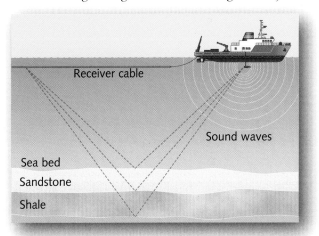

▲ Seismic surveying can detect different rock layers at sea.

When the sound waves travel through the ground they move through different rock layers at different speeds, and are refracted and reflected back to the surface in different ways. This means that it is possible to establish a picture of the structure of a cross-section of the ground. Scientists now know that different rocks tend to form layers, called 'strata', which can trap reserves of gas, oil and coal.

SEISMOLOGY

Seismology is similar to seismic surveying, but involves the detection of natural vibrations or sound waves in the ground, which are generated by the ground movements of earthquakes, tremors and volcanic eruptions. Ground movements occur when stresses that have built up are suddenly released as energy. This energy travels through the ground as sound waves because the Earth's crust is slightly elastic. Anything sitting on the crust becomes violently vibrated as the wave energy reaches the surface and gets absorbed by the environment. The very worst earthquakes release so much energy that they can be felt hundreds of kilometres away and towns and cities near the source can become totally destroyed in the process.

Seismology is used to predict and forewarn about these natural disasters. However, this is often very difficult because ground movements tend to happen suddenly and without warning. When an earthquake strikes, electronic devices (such as seismographs) can

▲ During an earthquake, sound waves travel underground at speeds of up to 15 kilometres per second.

be used to measure the effects. In 1935, US geologist Charles Richter devised a scale for measuring the intensity or amplitude of ground movements – known as the Richter scale. This is a logarithmic scale which means that 6 on the Richter scale is 10 times more powerful than 5 and 100 times more powerful than 4. The earthquake in Pakistan in 2005, for example, measured 7.6 on the Richter scale (the equivalent force of a nuclear bomb).

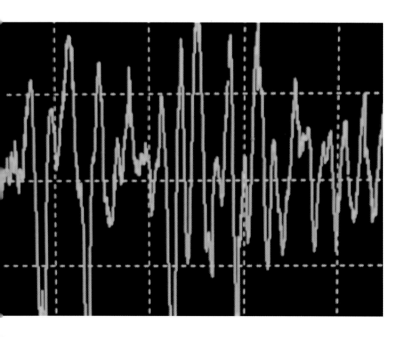

◀ Seismograph recordings show the intensity, direction and duration of shock waves following an earth tremor.

ULTRASOUND SCANNING

Some objects vibrate so quickly that the pitch (frequency) is too high for us to hear. These sounds are called 'ultrasounds' and can be used without causing discomfort to people's ears. Ultrasound scanning is also used to look inside the human body without causing any harm. In a similar way to sonar navigation or seismic surveying, ultrasound waves travel into the body and are refracted and reflected in different ways according to the types of tissue they encounter. The sound waves that return – echoes – are then converted into electrical signals and processed by a computer into a visual image. This method is especially useful for looking at unborn babies as they grow within their mothers' wombs.

ULTRASONIC TREATMENTS

Ultrasound scanning involves using high frequency sound waves with a relatively low strength or amplitude. If the amplitude is

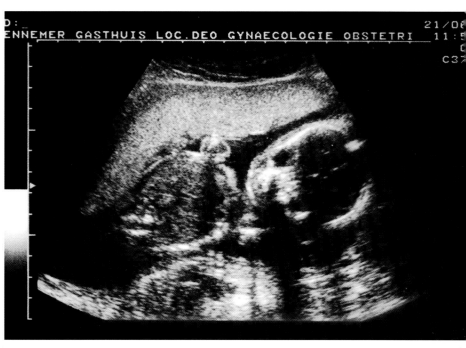

▲ Ultrasound scans can be used to show the development of an unborn child.

increased however, the sound waves carry more energy and can be used for some more advanced medical procedures. For example, gallstones (small stone-like calcium deposits within the gall bladder that can cause considerable pain) can be removed using **ultrasonic** sound waves.

Traditionally, gallstones were removed during an operation by cutting the gall bladder open and pulling the stones out using forceps. Today, however, instead of removing gallstones, it is possible to disintegrate them using high amplitude ultrasonic sound waves. Brittle objects, like gallstones, will crack and fall to pieces when exposed to ultrasonic sound, but soft body tissues are undamaged because they are flexible enough to absorb the energy of the sound waves. Once the gallstones have disintegrated they eventually find their way out of the body via the tubes that connect the gall bladder to the intestine.

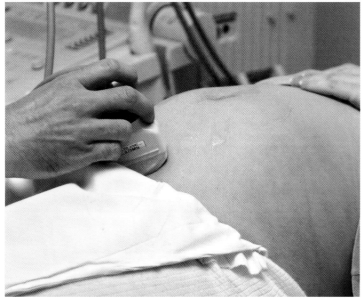

▲ This expectant mother is undergoing an ultrasound scan to check the health of her baby.

Another ultrasonic treatment uses a device called an ultrasonic probe. This device uses ultrasonic waves to numb nerve endings in the skin. It is used in preparation for injections or before inserting catheters or tracheotomy tubes, which are normally painful for the patient. Scientists have also gone one step further by administering drugs through the skin using ultrasound techniques. In the future this form of drug administration may replace painful injections and give a more gradual and natural dose of medication.

ULTRASONIC TOOLS

Ultrasound is inaudible to the human ear, and provides a cheap and safe alternative tool that can be used in manufacturing and industry. At extremely high levels of amplitude, ultrasonic waves can cause materials to heat up. This is particularly useful for soldering and welding metals and plastics, especially in situations where normal soldering and welding techniques are difficult to use or where the heat might cause damage to other components. Ultrasonic welders are used to connect lengths of plastic piping as they are being fed below the ground to achieve precise and watertight joins.

▲ This technician is using ultrasonic vibrations to check for cracks in the pipes of a chemical plant. If a fault is present, the device that he is holding will pick up the reflections of ultrasound waves.

Ultrasonic soldering irons can also melt solder at a precise point on a computer circuit board without exposing anything else to the heat. Ultrasound can be used for safety measures, too. At a chemical plant, technicians use ultrasound techniques to check the quality of pipes. This is important to prevent hazardous leaks. Faults, such as cracks, can be detected because they reflect the ultrasound waves.

TIME TRAVEL: INTO THE FUTURE

▶ Scientists have been exploring ways in which sound waves can be used to construct machinery in space. Tests onboard a space shuttle have shown that intense audible sounds can shape particles. One day this process – 'acoustic shaping' – could be used in space to build complex structures (such as space stations) saving considerable costs of transportation from Earth.

Reproducing sound

7

Humans communicate by making their own sounds, but they can also record sounds that can be played back at a later time, or in another location. Most recording technology is based on our knowledge of the human ear. Microphones and speakers, for example, have a diaphragm (rather like the eardrum) that is vibrated by sound waves. Recordings convert these sound waves into electrical signals that can be stored or transported and converted back into sounds again.

MICROPHONES

Microphones are used in many everyday appliances, such as telephones, tape recorders and radio and television broadcasting. Microphones contain a thin, flexible diaphragm that turns sound waves into physical vibrations and converts them into an electrical signal that can be encoded on a tape or CD. Some microphones need a power supply but others use an electromagnetic device that is activated when the diaphragm vibrates.

SPEAKERS

When CDs or tapes are played, the stored information is converted back into an electrical signal. A speaker then turns this signal back into physical vibrations. The sound waves are produced by rapidly vibrating a flexible cone (or diaphragm). The cone is usually made of paper, plastic or metal and is suspended so that it can move freely.

▲ A modern speaker.

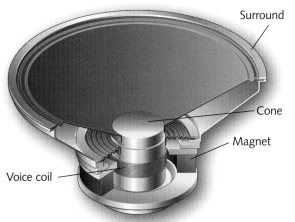

▲ The parts of a speaker used to produce sound waves.

Good quality speakers produce sound waves that are an exact replica of the original recording. Sound systems, with two or more speakers, work in stereo — each speaker converts slightly different electrical signals to give a more accurate representation of the original recording.

▲ This singer is using a microphone that sends electrical signals to an amplifier to make his voice louder.

Today, our world is full of sounds that entertain us. We play recorded music in our homes and we listen to live sounds on the radio. But it hasn't always been this way. The first machines that could be used in the home to reproduce recorded sounds arose in the late 1800s.

RECORD PLAYER

In 1877, Thomas Edison invented the first record player. It was called a phonograph – a small cylinder drum, covered with tin foil that had grooves scratched into its surface. These grooves were made using a recording needle attached to a 'voice catcher' that converted sound waves into vibrations. As the drum turned, the vibrations scratched a groove into the surface of the foil. When played back, variations in the groove caused a playing needle (or 'stylus') to vibrate. These vibrations were then converted into electrical signals, amplified and passed to loud speakers that converted them back into sound waves. However, the phonograph failed to sell commercially at the time because it was clumsy to use and easily damaged.

In 1886, Bell & Tainter invented an alternative version called the 'graphophone'. This cylinder was made of wax and produced a better sound. Then, in 1888, Emile Berliner's 'gramophone' used flat discs instead of cylinders. These discs began to be made from vinyl (a type of plastic) making it possible to record sound and also to make faithful copies of the original disc.

▲ Gramophones were a sophisticated phonograph and were commonly used until the early 1960s.

TAPE RECORDER

The first tape recorders were called wire recorders. They worked by fixing electrical signals from sound waves into a steel wire wound between spools. Wire recorders were used for telephone answering machines and dictaphones, but their recording quality was very poor. Then, in 1934, Joseph Begun invented the first magnetic tape recorder. Magnetic tape recorders use tape coated with fine particles of a magnetic substance which become magnetised by electrical signals that have been converted from sound waves using a microphone. The first magnetic tape recorders used spools of steel tape, making them extremely cumbersome to use. However, over the years, oxide-coated plastic tape improved the quality of the recorded sound and made tape recorders more practical. Then, the development of oxide-impregnated plastic film brought us the cassette tapes, video tapes and computer floppy discs that we still see today. In 1979, Sony produced the 'Walkman', a small, portable, battery-powered cassette player with earphones – a practical source of sound entertainment on the move.

▲ Tape recorders brought a practical way of making home recordings and a portable source of entertainment.

RADIO

The origins of the radio began in 1896 with the invention of wireless telegraphy by the Italian scientist Guglielmo Marconi. Marconi took the work of scientists like Hertz (see page 8) and began to experiment with ways of producing radio waves that could travel large distances. His work would later lead to radio transmission where sound waves are converted into electrical signals, via a microphone, and then converted into radio frequency waves that can travel long distances – to our homes or cars, for example.

▼ Radio frequency waves travel long distances making radios one of the most portable sound devices.

▲ In the 1930s, radios like this battery-operated Spartan model, brought music and broadcasts to many homes.

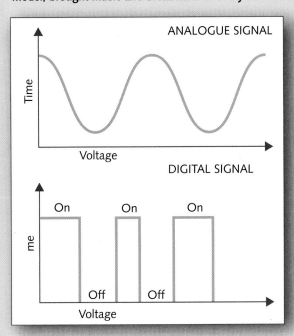

ANALOGUE SIGNAL

Time

Voltage

DIGITAL SIGNAL

On   On   On

me

Off   Off

Voltage

▲ An analogue signal is a continuous variable signal whereas a digital signal is a series of 'on' and 'off' pulses.

ANALOGUE TO DIGITAL

When sounds were originally recorded on tape or vinyl, the information was stored in a form called '**analogue**'. This meant that the sound waves were captured as a continuously variable signal. This worked well, but the quality of recordings soon deteriorated if secondary copies were made of copies of the original material.

A solution to this problem has been found in recording information in a new form called '**digital**'. In digital recordings, sound waves are captured in patterns of numbers (or code form), instead of an electrical signal. The technology is similar to that used in CD players. Digital radios produce a better sound quality and are largely immune to interference. Digital radios also offer additional features, such as multiple channels, flexible programme schedules and interactive features.

THE FUTURE OF SOUND RECORDING

The arrival of the compact disc (CD) in the early 1980s meant that sound storage was no longer physical (like vinyl records) or electromagnetic (like cassette tapes) but had become optical. Compact discs work by storing sounds as digital codes that are read by a laser beam. The combination of digital coding and laser meant that sounds could be recorded, stored and reproduced far more accurately than ever before. Soon the CD became even more compact when the mini-disc came on the market in 1992. At about six centimetres in diameter, mini discs are truly pocketsize. They store the same amount of sound recordings as a CD, but their smaller size makes them a much more practical storage solution.

▲ CDs and mini discs have increased the capacity of sound recordings that can be stored on a single disc.

◀ An MP3 player has enough storage for you to carry your music collection around with you.

The arrival of the MP3 in the late 1990s meant that storage capacity increased yet again. MP3s store sound information that has been compressed with little (or no) loss of sound quality. MP3 files reduce the size of audio data by up to 12 times. These files can be stored on a computer hard drive or in the memory chips of a portable MP3 player. This technology has changed the way in which people now carry their music collections. Instead of using multiple tapes or CDs, music can now be downloaded onto an MP3 player. Portable MP3 players can hold more than 1,000 songs and most have long-life batteries that last for up to 18 hours. MP3 files can also be downloaded from the internet, taking the sound recording phenomenon to a new level.

▶ Super audio CDs (SACDs) are soon to replace traditional CD sound recordings. Although similar to a CD in shape and size, SACDs have a superior way of storing and relaying digital sound. They use a similar technology to DVDs that are used to store digital video. SACDs can store about eight times as much data as a CD because the electrical signals are packed tightly together.

HYPERSONIC SOUND

Watch out for HyperSonic Sound (HSS) – a new technology that will revolutionise the way that we hear sound transmissions in the future. Just as a laser beam focuses light waves, HSS uses intensely focused sound waves that can travel long distances without dispersing. HSS technology uses two types of inaudible ultrasonic sound waves to carry sound data. This is similar to the way in which radio waves are used to carry sound waves (see page 41). Ultrasonic waves travel farther and stay more focused than lower frequency sound waves.

When the ultrasonic waves encounter an object, they slow down and bend, and as they crash together they re-create the original sound. A sound from an HSS speaker positioned 100 metres away will seem like it's coming through headphones because the sound is being created next to you. The signals also reflect off surfaces – some noises may seem to come from a different direction.

▲ HyperSonic Sound could be used on aircraft carriers where it is difficult to hear instructions above the noise.

Although we are unlikely to see HyperSonic Sound technology being used for some years, it has enormous potential. An HSS-equipped car could play one CD for passengers in the front and another for passengers in the back. HSS speakers could be used at stations and airports to make travel announcements for the sole attention of appropriate passengers. Police teams could also use the technology as a non-violent weapon in raids or to disperse riot crowds with the use of 'sonic bullets' – painful bursts of sound that exceed the human pain threshold. The fact that HSS can be reflected could also be useful to distract criminals with a sound when storming a building from a different direction. It is early days for HyperSonic Sound but the technology is set to become increasingly common in the coming years.

▲ If you step out of an HSS beam, the ultrasonic waves move silently past because they have nothing to collide with.

The one communication device that has revolutionised the lives of ordinary people is the telephone. We can talk to people many thousands of kilometres away thanks to this piece of equipment. Telephones convert sound waves into electrical signals that travel along wires or cables before they are converted back into a tone that sounds like the original voice. A number of scientists were involved in developing the various components that make up the telephone. For example, in 1831, the English scientist Michael Faraday proved that vibrations of metal could be converted into electrical impulses. Later in 1861, a German named Johann Reis built a simple apparatus that changed sound waves into electricity and back again.

Two men then actually invented the telephone independently (Elisha Gray from the USA and Alexander Graham Bell from Scotland, UK). Gray built the first telephone receiver in 1874 but he wasn't able to master the design of a workable

▲ A replica of Bell's first telephone – the Gallows telephone (1875). This experimental telephone could transmit sounds, but could not receive them.

transmitter until after Bell's efforts in 1876. Just as your eardrum is pushed back and forth by sound waves, Bell's telephone mouthpiece had a diaphragm that moved. This converted the sound waves from a voice into electrical signals that travelled along a cable to a second telephone, where they were fed into a speaker in the earpiece. The speaker then converted the electrical signals back into sound waves that could be heard by the recipient. In essence, the telephone still works in exactly the same way, although the electrical signals are now often converted into digital signals, which travel as radio waves (in mobile phones) or as optical pulses between telephone exchanges (for landlines).

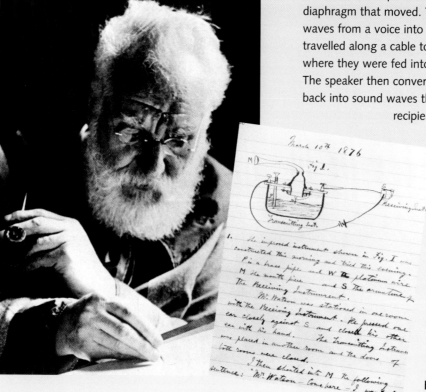

◀ Alexander Bell and a notebook entry in which he describes the invention of his first telephone.

▲ Call centres enable companies to increase their business by taking billions of phone calls every year.

MOBILE TELEPHONES

Mobile telephones have become an indispensable part of our everyday lives. In Europe and the USA, around 70 per cent of the population now own a mobile phone. But how do they work?

It was only natural that telephone and radio technology would eventually be combined. Mobile telephones, invented by the Bell Telephone Company, are actually a type of radio. They were originally used in New York police cars in the 1920s, and received radio signals from one antenna in the city. However, the mobile phones that we are familiar with, would not become common for another four decades.

Until 1987, mobile phones were large and clumsy and they used analogue technology. Speech was converted into an electrical signal and – in a similar way to radio technology – the telephones transmitted and received signals on a particular frequency. The calls were expensive because only a limited number of people could use each frequency at any one time. However, in the late 1980s, digital technology overcame these problems. Today, mobile phones can be used over longer distances. There is one major

▶ Increasing mobile phone technology is now combining sound transmission with text messages, cameras and the internet.

digital network – GSM – that caters for more than 70 per cent of digital mobile phone users worldwide. In Europe, GSM mobiles send and receive data over radio waves at around 900 or 1,800 MHz, and in the USA, the frequency is around 1,900 MHz. The digital network is divided into a patchwork of 'cells' to avoid restrictions on the number of people that can use a frequency. Each cell has a base station that transmits and receives signals using a handful of the network's frequencies. People in different cells can use the same frequencies without their calls interfering. In rural areas, high-power base stations are used to produce cells that provide coverage of up to a 20-kilometre radius. In urban areas, low-power base stations produce smaller cells that usually cover a 50 to 300-metre radius. Sometimes, a call has to move between cells as the user moves around. The phone constantly monitors the signals of neighbouring cells and switches to receive the best signal possible.

Digital mobile networks were designed to carry voice communications, but they now carry other forms of data, too. Text messaging has become very popular and despite the phone's tiny screens, it is also possible to access internet pages from some mobile phones. As the technology develops, some mobiles have a microphone that detects a person's voice through the vibrations of the bones in their head. These all-in-one mobile phone headsets have a microphone in the earpiece.

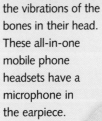

Glossary

ACOUSTICS – The scientific study of sound. In particular, the production, transmission and reception of sound.

AMPLITUDE – The strength of volume of a signal. When a sound is amplified, it gets louder.

ANALOGUE – Analogue is a term used to describe the representation of an object that resembles the original event. An analogue signal, such as a radio wave, is a continuously variable signal that goes up and down with the loudness of the sound. Televisions, radios, tape recorders and some telephones use analogue signals, although they are beginning to be replaced by digital signals. This is because analogue signals tend to be affected by electrical interference.

AQUATIC – Related to water. Aquatic plants or animals grow or live in (or near) water.

ASYMMETRICAL – To have a lack of symmetry (or balance).

COMPRESSION – To squeeze together. In the movement of sound waves, compression is followed by rarefraction (moving apart).

DIGITAL – A digital signal is a signal transmitted in code format, rather than as a continuously variable signal. Mobile telephones use digital signals. Other devices to join the digital revolution are radios, televisions and the internet (broadband). Digital signals produce a better reception than analogue signals and are also more versatile.

ECHO – The repetition of a sound caused by the reflection of sound waves from a surface.

INSULATION – The use of materials or devices to prevent sound, heat or electricity travelling through a medium.

INVERTEBRATES – Animals that do not have a backbone or spinal column.

LONGITUDINAL – A term to describe a movement that is 'back to front' or 'top to bottom'. Longitudinal is the opposite of 'transverse'.

MAMMALS – Warm-blooded animals that have a backbone or spinal column and milk-producing mammary glands (in the female) for nourishing the young.

ANSWERS

p24 Investigate
The speed of sound is 340 metres per second.

p25 Test yourself
(1) It is not possible for sound waves to travel through a vacuum because they need a material, such as air, in which to travel. There are no particles in a vacuum.

(2) We see the flash of lightning before we hear the sound of thunder because light travels faster than sound. Light travels at about 300,000 km per second. Sound travels at about 340 m per second (in air).

(3) From fastest to slowest: Wood, water, hydrogen. The closer the atoms are arranged in a material (through which a sound is travelling), the faster the sound waves move.

p30 Test yourself
From high to low – violin, viola, cello. The following factors change the pitch of the note: the size and shape of the instrument; the thickness of the strings; the length of the strings; the tension of the strings.

OSCILLOSCOPE – An electronic device, used to provide a visual display of electrical signals. If sound waves are converted into electrical signals they can be displayed on an oscilloscope. The device clearly shows the length (frequency) and height (amplitude) of each sound wave.

PITCH – The tone of a note. Pitch is determined by the frequency of a sound wave.

RAREFRACTION – When particles move further away from one another. In the movement of sound waves, rarefraction is followed by compression.

REFLECTION – When sound (or light) waves strike a surface and travel back again.

REFRACTION – The turning or bending of a sound (or light) wave when it passes from one medium into another, of a different density.

RESONANCE – When a sound is intense and prolonged it is said to have resonance.

SEISMOLOGY – The study of earthquakes and related issues.

SONAR – A technique that uses reflected underwater sound waves to detect and locate submerged objects or to measure the depths of a body of water, such as the ocean. Sonar stands for 'sound navigation and ranging'.

SONIC BOOM – An explosive sound caused by a shock wave that is produced by an object moving through the air faster than the speed of sound.

SOUNDING – To measure the depth of water. Rods and lines can be used for sounding. Today however, echoes are more commonly used for sounding techniques.

SOUNDPROOF – To make sounds inaudible. The rooms of a home are often soundproofed by using insulating materials, such as fibreglass, that absorb sound waves.

STEREOPHONIC – When sounds come from two (or more) different directions. We have two ears that receive sound waves at different times, helping us to detect sounds from all around us. Stereophonic recorded sounds use two (or more) channels so that sounds have a more realistic effect.

SUPERSONIC – Faster than the speed of sound.

TRANSVERSE – A term to describe a movement that is 'side to side'. The opposite of 'longitudinal'.

ULTRASONIC – Frequencies that are inaudible to the human ear. Ultrasonic sounds are above approximately 20,000 hertz.

ULTRASOUND – A medical technique that uses high frequency sound waves to produce images of the organs and structure of the body. Ultrasound 'echo' images can be viewed on a monitor when sound waves are reflected from tissues within the body. Ultrasound is used to monitor the development of an unborn child because the sound waves are not harmful.

VACUUM – A space that does not contain any matter. Sound waves cannot travel in a vacuum.

VIBRATE – To move rapidly (from side to side, to or fro, or up and down).

Useful websites:
www.bbc.co.uk/schools
www.popsci.com
www.sciencenewsforkids.org
www.newscientist.com
www.howstuffworks.com

Index

PHOTO CREDITS – (abbv: r, right, l, left, t, top, m, middle, b, bottom) **Cover background image** Giansanti/Corbis Sygma **Front cover images** (r) Gabe Palmer/Corbis (l) Andrew Brookes/Corbis **Back cover image** (inset) Andrew Brookes/Corbis **p.1** (tr) Carlos Munoz-Yague/Eurelios/Science Photo Library **p.1** (bl) www.istockphoto.com (br) Bob Winsett/Corbis **p.2** (bl) Andrew Brookes/Corbis **p.3** (tr) www.istockphoto.com/Paul Piebinga (br) John D. Norman/Corbis **p.4** (tl) Corbis (tr) Bo Veisland/Science Photo Library (bl) Peter Turnley/Corbis (br) www.istockphoto.com/Ben Renard-Wiart **p.5** www.istockphoto.com/Paul Cowan **p.6** (l) www.istockphoto.com/Arlindo Silva **p.7** (t) Neal Grundy/Science Photo Library (bl) John D. Norman/Corbis (br) www.istockphoto.com/Karen Winton **p.8** (l) Andrew Brookes/Corbis (r) www.istockphoto.com/Paul Cowan **p.9** (t) www.istockphoto.com/Bjarne Kvaale (b) Gabe Palmer/Corbis **p.10** (tr) Corbis (m) Science Photo Library **p.11** (bl) Macduff Everton/Corbis **p.13** (br) Bo Veisland/Science Photo Library **p.14** (tr) Steve Gschmeissner/Science Photo Library **p.15** (t) www.istockphoto.com/Joe Stone (b) Jonathan Blair/Corbis **p.16** (tr) www.istockphoto.com/Laurie Knight (bl) www.istockphoto.com/Ben Renard-Wiart **p.17** (tr) www.istockphoto.com/Clayton Hansen (br) www.istockphoto.com/Dirk Conradt **p.18** (tr) Bo Veisland/Science Photo Library (bl) Howard Davies/Corbis **p.19** (b) Peter Turnley/Corbis **p.20** (tm) Science Photo Library (mr) Will & Deni McIntyre/Corbis (bl) Prof. Peter Fowler/Science Photo Library (br) TopFoto.co.uk/HIP **p.21** (b) Mauro Fermasiello/Science Photo Library **p.22** John Madere/Corbis **p.23** (t) US Department of Defence/Science Photo Library (b) Richard. T. Nowitz/Corbis **p.24** (l) Bob Rowan; Progressive Image/Corbis **p.25** (tr) www.istockphoto.com/Paige Falk (br) C.S Langlois, Publiphoto Diffusion/Science Photo Library **p.26** (t) Science Photo Library (b) T F Letocha, pixelSnaps **p.27** (br) BSIP Laurent Caby/Science Photo Library **p.28** (t) TopFoto.co.uk/Keystone (ml) Robert & Linda Mostyn; Eye Ubiquitous/Corbis **p.29** (t) Corbis **p.30** (tl) www.istockphoto.com/Nicholas Sutcliffe (tr) The SoundJunction project of the Associated Board of the Royal Schools of Music (www.soundjunction.org) (b) Bob Winsett/Corbis **p.31** (b) www.istockphoto.com **p.33** (tr) European Parliament (b) www.istockphoto.com/Leigh Schindler **p.34** (tr) www.istockphoto.com/Raymond Truelove (bl) www.istockphoto.com **p.35** (bl) Alexis Rosenfield/Science Photo Library **p.36** (tr) Carl Frank/Science Photo Library (b) Carlos Munoz-Yague/Eurelios/Science Photo Library **p.37** (tr) www.istockphoto.com/Dirk Conradt **p.38** (tr) Milan Radulovic **p.38** Maximilian Stock Ltd/Science Photo Library **p.39** (tr) www.istockphoto.com/Jostein Hauge (bl) www.sxc.hu/Norbert Machinek **p.40** (tr) Victor de Schwanberg/Science Photo Library (bl) www.istockphoto.com **p.41** (tr) Emely/zefa/Corbis (tl) www.istockphoto.com/Don Wilkie **p.42** (tr) www.freeimages.co.uk (bl) www.sxc.hu/Jannes **p.43** (tr) Master Sgt. Jack Braden/US Air Force (bl) www.istockphoto. com/Paul Piebinga **p.44** (tr) The Telephone Museum, Milton Keynes Museum (bl) Library of Congress/Science Photo Library (bm) Library of Congress/Science Photo Library **p.45** (tl) Corbis (br) www.sxc.hu/Richard Mallinson